# Into Scie

# time

## Terry Jennings

## Illustrations by David Anstey

## Oxford

Published by Oxford University Press, Walton Street, Oxford OX2 6DP
Oxford New York Toronto
Delhi Bombay Calcutta Madras Karachi
Petaling Java Singapore Hong Kong Tokyo
Nairobi Dar es Salaam Cape Town
Melbourne Auckland

and associated companies in
Beirut Berlin Ibadan Nicosia

Oxford is a trade mark of Oxford University Press

First Published 1988
Reprinted 1990

Reading Consultant: Norman Ruel
(formerly Head of Teaching and Support Service, Reading, Berkshire).

**British Library Cataloguing in Publication Data**

Jennings, Terry, 1938–
Time
1. Time — For children
I. Title     II. Anstey, David
529

ISBN 0-19-918258-2
ISBN 0-19-918252-3 pbk

This book was designed and produced by BLA Publishing Limited,
TR House, Christopher Road, East Grinstead, Sussex, England.

A member of the **Ling Kee Group**
LONDON·HONG KONG·TAIPEI·SINGAPORE·NEW YORK

Phototypeset in Britain by BLA Publishing/Composing Operations
Colour origination by Planway Limited
Printed and bound in Great Britain by MacLehose and Partners Ltd, Portsmouth

What time did you get up this morning?
What time did you come to school?
When do you have lunch?
What time will you have tea?
What time will you go to bed?
Caroline made a picture clock.
What time did she do these different things?

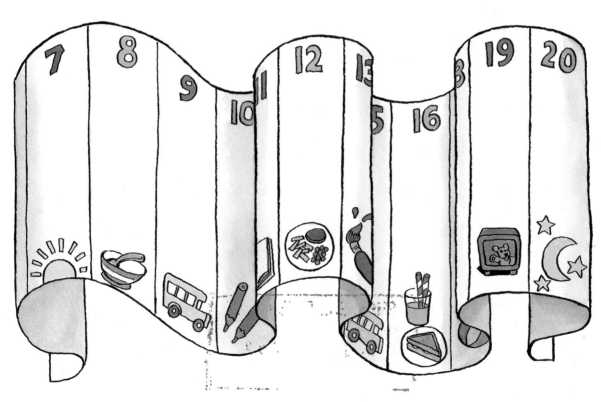

Some clocks and watches have hands.
The hands move to show the time.
Some clocks and watches have
only numbers.
The numbers move to show the time.
Some clocks and watches are worked
by electricity.
The electricity comes from a battery
or from a plug in the wall.
In some clocks and watches a spring
moves the hands.
From time to time the spring has
to be wound up.
Look at the pictures.
All of these objects measure the time.
What are these objects used for?
What moves the hands or numbers?

4

Early one morning David stood
on the playground.
Anna drew around his feet with chalk.
Anna also drew around David's shadow.
The shadow was long.
At lunchtime, David stood in the same place.
Anna again drew around David's shadow.
The shadow had moved and it was
much shorter.
At home-time, David stood on the playground.
Do you think his shadow had moved again?
Was the shadow long or short?

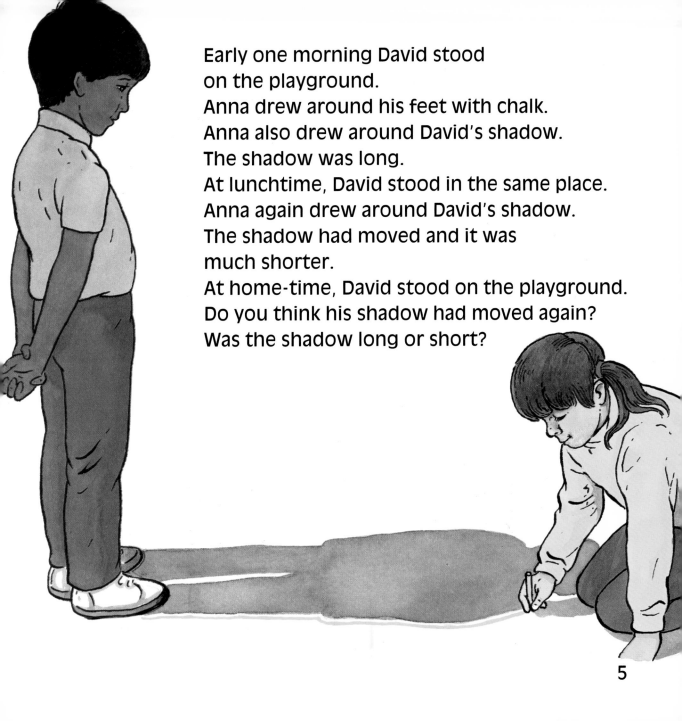

This is a sundial.
Some large gardens have sundials.
Some churches have sundials.
A sundial can tell you the time.
The pointer on the sundial
makes a shadow when the
sun shines.
The shadow is in the same
place at the same time each day.
You can tell the time with
the sundial on a sunny day.
Could you tell the time with
a sundial at night?

William made a sundial.
He pushed a stick into the lawn.
He did not move the stick at all.
At 9 o'clock William looked for the shadow
of the stick.
He marked the end of the shadow with a pebble.
At 10 o'clock the shadow had moved.
Had the stick moved?
William marked the end of the shadow
with another pebble.
Was the shadow in the same place
at 11 o'clock?
How could William use his stick
to tell the time?

7

This is an egg-timer.
It has sand in it.
An egg-timer is really
a sand clock.
It tells you how long
to boil an egg.
You boil an egg until all
the sand has run from
the top to the bottom.

Caroline made a sand clock.
She took a clean dry plastic bottle.
Caroline's teacher cut the bottom off the bottle.

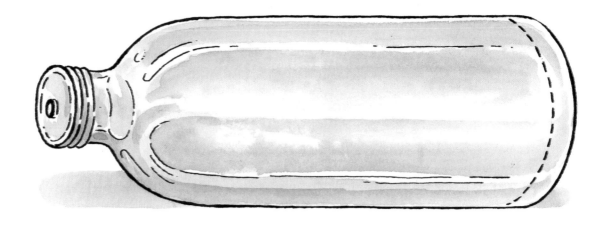

Caroline stood the bottle in a jar like this.
The jar had a strip of paper stuck on it.
There were lines on the paper.
Caroline filled the bottle with fine
dry sand.
She stood the bottle upside down
over the jar.
Caroline counted slowly until the
sand got to the first line.
How could she use her sand clock
to time an egg?
What else could Caroline have
used in her clock besides sand?

9

David made a water clock.
He had a clean plastic cup.
He made a tiny hole in the bottom
of the cup with a pin.
David stood the cup on top
of a jar like this.
He filled the cup with water.
He then counted slowly, 1, 2, 3, 4 ...
David had counted to 18 when
the water reached the
first line on the paper.
He counted another 21 before
the water reached the next line
on the paper.
Why was there a difference?
Make your own water clock.
Time some things with
your clock.

Anna also made a water clock.
Her water clock was different from David's.
Anna nailed together two pieces of wood
like this.
She found six plastic cups.
She made a tiny hole in the bottom of five
of them.
Anna used drawing pins to fix the cups
to the upright piece of wood.
She put the cup without a hole in it
at the bottom.

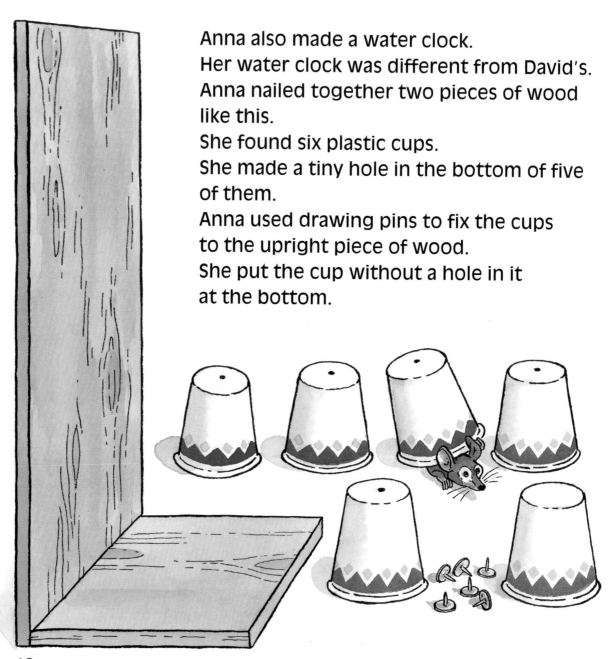

Anna filled the top cup with water.
She used a watch with a second hand.
Anna saw how long it took for all
the water to reach the bottom cup.
Did it take more or less time than
David's water clock?

13

William made a candle clock.
He measured a candle.
He stood it up in plasticine in a metal tray.
William's teacher lit the candle for him.
William let it burn for 10 minutes.
Then he blew the candle out and
measured it again.
The candle had burned 1 centimetre
in 10 minutes.

William drew lines on the rest of the candle.
He made the lines 1 centimetre apart.
William put a pin in each of the lines.
His teacher lit the candle again.
What happened when the candle burned down
1 centimetre?
How much longer did the candle last?

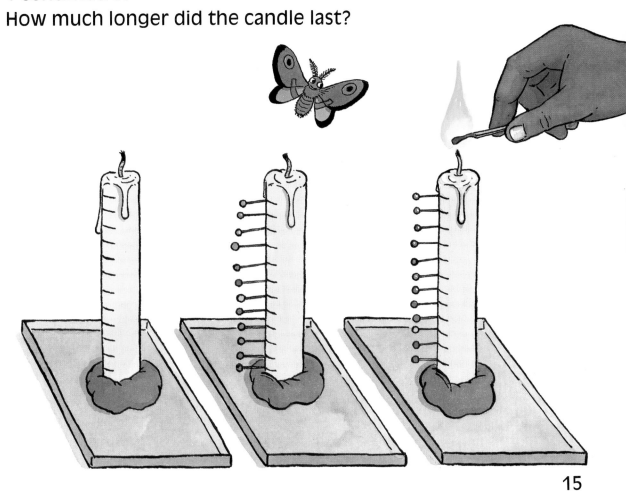

Caroline has an alarm clock.
It rings when it is time
for her to get up.
The alarm clock rings at the
time it was set to ring.
When does Caroline's alarm
clock ring?

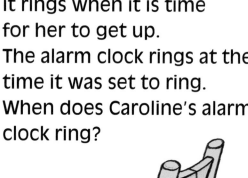

candle  pin

thread

plasticine

marble

David made his own alarm clock.
This is a picture of it.
Can you say how David's alarm
clock worked?
Did David's alarm clock ring?
Is there an alarm clock in your
home?
Are there any other clocks
which ring when they were
set to ring?

16

All clocks and watches show hours and minutes.
Some also show how many seconds have gone by.
This clock has three hands.
The red one is called a second hand.
It shows how many seconds have gone by.
It takes 60 seconds, or 1 minute, for the hand
to go right round.
Look at a clock with a second hand.
How many times can you bounce a ball in 30 seconds?
How many seconds does it take you to drink a glass of water?

17

David made a pendulum.
He tied a weight to a piece of string.
David tied the string to a drawing pin
in a piece of wood.
He started the pendulum swinging.
David counted how many times
the pendulum swung to and fro.
The pendulum swung 15 times in
10 seconds.
David made the string longer.
He swung the pendulum again.
This time it swung 10 times in
10 seconds.
David then made the string very long.
He swung the pendulum again.
How many swings do you think
it made?
Was it more or less than before?
David made a pendulum with a heavy
weight on it.
Did it swing faster or slower than
before?

This is an old clock.
It is called a grandfather clock.
A pendulum makes the grandfather
clock keep the correct time.
The pendulum swings backwards
and forwards.
But the pendulum does not move
on its own.
The pendulum is moved by
a heavy weight.
The weight slowly falls as the
pendulum swings.
After a few days the weight has to
be lifted up again.
The weight is lifted by winding it up
with a key.

Anna wanted to listen to her heart.
She wanted to hear it beating.
She had a short piece of rubber tube and two plastic funnels.
Anna fixed the funnels to the tube like this.
She put one funnel over her heart.
She put the other funnel to her ear.
Anna counted how fast her heart was beating.
Her heart beat 90 times in a minute.
Would her heart beat faster or slower if Anna ran?

bean seedling

William thinks that plants can tell the time.
Every morning the daisy flowers in his garden open.
They close up every evening.
They stay closed until the next morning.
William planted a runner bean seed.
The seed grew into a bean seedling.
This is what the seedling looked like during the day.
This is what it looked like every evening.
What differences can you see?
Do you think that plants can tell the time?

22

# glossary

Here are the meanings of some words which you might have met for the first time in this book.

**alarm clock**: a clock which rings at the set time.

**battery**: a device for storing and supplying electricity.

**clock**: an instrument for measuring and showing the passage of time.

**egg-timer**: a sand clock which is used to show how long it takes to boil an egg.

**pendulum**: a swinging wire or rod with a weight on the end.

**second**: a unit of time. Sixty seconds make one minute.

**seed**: a small part of a plant which can be sown to produce a new plant.

**seedling**: a young plant.

**shadow**: the dark shape which appears on the ground or on a wall when an object is between it and the light.

**spring**: a springy device made of a coil of metal or wire.

**sundial**: a device which shows the time by a shadow cast by the sun.

# index